Mindfulness for Busy Moms

A Simple Guide to Reducing Stress and Living a Happier Life

© **Copyright 2018 - All rights reserved.**

The content contained within this book may not be reproduced, duplicated or transmitted without direct written permission from the author or the publisher.

Under no circumstances will any blame or legal responsibility be held against the publisher, or author, for any damages, reparation, or monetary loss due to the information contained within this book. Either directly or indirectly.

Legal Notice:

This book is copyright protected. This book is only for personal use. You cannot amend, distribute, sell, use, quote or paraphrase any part, or the content within this book, without the consent of the author or publisher.

Disclaimer Notice:

Please note the information contained within this document is for educational and entertainment purposes only. All effort has been executed to present accurate, up to date, and reliable, complete information. No warranties of any kind are declared or implied. Readers acknowledge that the author is not engaging in the rendering of legal, financial, medical or professional advice. The content within this book has been derived from various sources. Please consult a licensed professional before attempting any techniques outlined in this book.

ISBN-13: 978-1720922865

Table of Contents

Preface 1
   How to Use this Book 2

Chapter 1: Introduction 3
   What is Mindfulness? 3
   Benefits of Mindfulness 5

Chapter 2: How to be Mindful 9
   Steps in Being Mindful 11

Chapter 3: Awareness of your Thoughts and Feelings 19
   Emotional Awareness 20
   Here are some of the techniques
   to be aware of in our thoughts and feelings. 22

Chapter 4: Meditation 29
   Sitting 30
   How to Sit? 30
   Types of Mindful Meditation
   Techniques to Practice at Home 33

Chapter 5: Mindful Acceptance 37
   How to Practice Mindful Acceptance 39
   Ways to Cultivate Mindful Acceptance 40

    Importance of Mindful Acceptance 42

Chapter 6: Gratitude and Joy 45
    Cultivating Joy 48

Chapter 7: Supporting Others 53

Chapter 8: Practicing Compassion 57
    The connection between Mindfulness
    and Compassion 58
    How to Practice Compassion as a Mother 60

Chapter 9: Dealing with Stress 65
    How to Mindfully Meditate to Solve your Stress 73
    Tips to Help Remain Calm when Dealing
    with Your Difficult Child 74

Chapter 10: Managing Anger 81
    Using Mindfulness to Control Your Anger 82

Chapter 11: Meaning and Purpose of Life 89
    Using Mindfulness to Discover the Purpose
    of your Life 91

Conclusion 93
    How to Start Being Mindful Today 93
    How to Create Habits of Mindfulness
    and Meditation and Stick to Them 95
    Mindful Things to do Everyday 97

Bonus 101

PREFACE

Busy moms undergo a lot of pressure while trying to raise their children, and at the same time concentrating on their often demanding careers. Although most moms may comfortably cater for their families through their careers, many are not happy due to a stressful and overwhelming life experiences. Their life is in constant motion and they feel like their days run together on autopilot mode. Imagine working outside home, trying to be a good mom, trying to take care of themselves, catering for their families. It can really be demanding and stressful. As moms undergo this crazy stressful life, trying to focus on their career growth and at the same time correctly raising their children, it is essential to practice mindfulness by incorporating it in their daily life. Additionally, moms should raise their children in a mindful way as it's important for their mental health.

How to Use this Book

This book can easily be used by busy moms, not only to learn mindfulness but to also incorporate it in their daily busy lives. This book employs simple, understandable language with real life examples on how to be mindful during activities such as driving, laundry, breakfast, and showering. The book will also teach you about meditation and how to manage stress and anger in the daily life of a busy mom. Just read through, understand, and practice the ideas in the book in your real life, as they will definitely help you to be mindful.

CHAPTER ONE

INTRODUCTION

What is Mindfulness?

Mindfulness is a state of being fully aware of what is going in the moment without having to wish for a change of that particular state or fearing that the state you are in won't change. Mindfulness also refers to the act of listening carefully to your feelings and thoughts at the moment. It involves pushing the "stop button" and thinking critically about our actions or whatever is happening around us and assessing the validity of our feelings and thoughts.

When we are mindful, we can make wiser choices and take things a little bit less personally. Being mindful will help you soothe your screaming toddler as they throw things at you, and to remain calm even when your six-year-old daughter decorates the home with Sharpies. Mindfulness will enable you to be more joyful in all the moments of bringing up your children, coupled with a demanding career.

Most moms think that it's impossible to become more mindful especially in tough life situations where they might be struggling to stay afloat. What they may not know is that mindfulness may just be the solution to their problems and enable them to float over the problems they may be facing. Learning to practice mindfulness in our lives and becoming more mindful doesn't require you to study Buddhism or spend days studying yoga. What you need to do to be mindful in your life is to practice approaching every life situation with an open intention, coupled with a great awareness of your every action. The difference between an agitated, petulant mom and a calm, gratified mom is a daily routine incorporating mindfulness into their daily lives.

Benefits of Mindfulness

Mindfulness is so beneficial for busy moms that global corporations, notably Google, are training their employees with it as it has been proven productive. At times when life becomes overwhelming due to different situations we face as busy moms, mindfulness becomes very helpful in solving such situations. Here are some of the benefits of mindfulness for a busy mom.

1. Mindfulness Creates an Authentic and Trusting Connection

Mindfulness enables you to focus entirely on the children without judging them on their actions. This enables your child to open, as they will know you are there for them, listening, watching and loving them for who they are. By doing this, your child will be able to feel safe in their attachment to you and you will remain fulfilled by them.

2. Empathy and Understanding

In being present with your child and seeing who your child is authentically, you will begin to share in their emotion. You will understand their curiosity, the way they see the world with splendor and amazement, their pace.

And in joining them in this beautiful child-world, you begin to empathize with them, their joy, their frustration, their laughter, their tears. This too builds a stronger relationship.

3. Gratitude for the moment

Joining your child in-the-moment, in their world, offers you the opportunity to simply BE in the moment, and to let go of all your external pressures and demands. You are fully connected with your child and therefore feel no rush, but rather a sense of gratitude for the gift of the moment.

4. Compassion & Patience

In these moments, the triggers of impatience – anxiety about the future or preconditioning/regrets about the past

– do not come into play. And so, you interact from a place of infinite patience with them, simply being in the now. Once you are in a place of deep and empathetic connection with your child, you are instinctively guided to act and communicate out of love and compassion. This helps us to manage our children's "mistakes" without judgment and with a learning-orientated perspective.

5. Awareness & Self-confidence

As we model active, compassionate listening to our child's essence, they too learn to respect their true SELVES – their instincts, their passions, their vitality. They become aware of their inner voice and with self-respect, they too grow self-confident in their choices and decisions. And as they learn to relate to themselves in this way, they will also learn to relate to others around them as well. Meanwhile, for us, practicing mindfulness helps us to alter our habitual responses by taking pause and choosing how we act. When we are mindful, we experience our life as we live it. We experience the world directly through our five senses. We recognize the thoughts we are having. In doing so, we learn how our minds work, and we are better able to label our thoughts and feelings we are having, instead of allowing them to overpower us and dictate our behavior.

CHAPTER TWO

HOW TO BE MINDFUL

As we discussed in the previous chapter, mindfulness enables us to calm down when we are caught up in stressful life moments i.e. when our kids are being grumpy at us or refusing to get out of bed. They're building anger and frustrations in us. Mindfulness enables us to be less reactive with our husbands, kids, co-workers, and ourselves. Mindfulness is the state of non-judgmental moment-to-moment awareness. The key to being mindful is to eliminate the judgment of our thoughts and feelings before acting on a given subject. As soon as we judge our thoughts, we multiply our feelings and pass them to those surrounding us in the form of anger or frustration.

Mindfulness in your life is not an overnight activity. It is challenging to be understood and incorporated into our daily busy life. It should be enjoyable and effortless as it comes naturally with time. By becoming mindful, you should stop overthinking both externally (external conscience) and internally and become real silent-cessation of both thinking by our mind and talking with our mouths. This kind of silence does not oppress us but rather nourishes and heals as it's a powerfully elegant sound.

Mindfulness is similar to concentration, as they are both sources of happiness and joy. Mindful energy is combined with the energy of concentration in your mind. For instance, when you are conscious of a certain object, let's say a car, and maintain your consciousness on that particular object, it will be said that you are concentrating on the car. The power of concentration increases proportionally with your mindfulness power. In full concentration, you are able to figure out a certain problem and come up with an applicable solution.

At first, being mindful may prove difficult and doesn't guarantee a 100% success rate, but you shouldn't give up at the first encounter as it is a slow and adaptive process. It is important to note that mindfulness cannot be mastered in a day, but with time and patience, it will become part of your everyday life. Mindfulness has positively impacted the lives of many moms and it can impact your life by applying the following techniques in your daily life as a busy mom.

Steps in Being Mindful

1. Focus on the Breath

This is one of the easiest technique to be mindful. You simply stop what you are doing and focus on the feeling in your stomach, along with the rising and falling of the chest as you exhale and inhale through your nostrils. Breathing correctly has been scientifically proven to lower blood pressure, which rises with frustration or anger and eliminates anxiety, helping you to focus and concentrate. You don't need to change your breathing tempo, just close your eyes and take four to five deep breaths through your nostrils and out through the mouth. Always inhale and exhale four to five times when overwhelmed or frazzled and every morning after you have woken up thinking about the day's activities.

2. Beware of your Surroundings

Your surroundings dictate your thoughts and feelings. You can slow your racing thoughts by observing your surroundings, as it can help slow them down. By observing your surroundings, your brain is diverted from overconcentration, and you will be doing something in place of obsessing. When we try to locate more than five things in our surrounding, we divert our attention and minimize thinking of our current situation. Peaceful observation will reconnect you with your environment.

Idea

You can place flowers on the kitchen table to slow down the race of your thoughts, keep you calm, and make you happy. Even with the chaos and clutter around the house with kids, the flowers bring everything to a relaxed level.

3. Live in the Moment

Living in the moment (moment awareness) is a key component of being mindful. As a busy mom, you can easily be carried away thinking of upcoming schedules, milestones, and other chores. Mindfulness will enable you to be aware of present happenings, which are important for the safety of your child, which is your responsibility as a mother. Trying to be aware of your current situation, such as when you are driving, playing with the baby, or even showering the baby. By living in the moment, you can be mindful of current activities.

4. Express Gratitude

Before waking up to handle the day's activities, always think of five to ten things you are grateful for. Think of where you started, how you are blessed with a beautiful family, an outstanding career, and how lucky you may be. You might also keep reminding yourself of such things throughout the day in every stressful situation you may be experiencing. Habitual gratitude meditations will enable you to be mindful of current situation by giving you a brighter view of your life as a busy mom.

5. Perform a Virtual Body Examination

Always take time from your daily routine and lie down to perform a body scan, examining your body from the toes up to your head, checking each part of your magnificent body virtually. By doing this, you are bringing awareness to your body and will easily maintain a state of being mindful. You may try this practice daily before you get out of bed or just right before you sleep, and you will definitely see changes in practicing mindfulness in your daily life.

6. Discharge Accumulated Tension

In our daily lives as busy moms, we experience building up the tension by nerve-wracking on several issues such as the safety of our children, career deadlines, and other worries moms experience. Accumulation of these tensions lead to stress and depression, putting us in a state of absent-mindedness, which is dangerous for our kids.

You can release tension by scanning your body, then massage your muscles by giving each muscle a perfect squeeze, then release from head to toe. You can also unclench your teeth to release the tension held in our jaws. You may also visit a spa and discharge accumulated tension by getting a proper massage, and you will feel your stress and depression dissolve, enabling you to be mindful.

7. *Engage in a Mindful Walk.*

Busy moms should occasionally take a mindful walk away from their busy schedules as it's helpful in redistributing your concentration about certain stressful issues, thereby significantly cutting your stress levels and enabling you to be mindful. You may also want to walk with your children by strapping them to the stroller, as you will be exposing your kid to the surrounding environment and at the same time enabling you to be mindful. A stroller will make you walk slower than usual, helping you to concentrate on other things such as the steps you make, nature, your child's looks, and numerous other small details. Additionally, you will be exposing your toddler to sunlight, which is essential for the synthesis of vitamin D important for bone development, and developing your baby's language at the same time. Just make sure not to overexpose your baby to the sun's rays, as they cause skin cancer.

8. Become Less Judgmental

By being nonjudgmental, you can forgive yourself and your family when they mess up, and be kind to yourself, making you mindful. You can handle a situation more calmly and composed when you are less judgmental compared to when you are extremely judgmental on miniature non-issues. Instead of judging your family and workmates, just note down your thoughts and feelings about a certain subject or occurrences and practice mindfulness by living in the moment and letting out your feelings and thoughts.

You may also let your feelings or thoughts pass over without having to judge those involved, whether it be your kids, husband, family, or even workmates. You will be able to be a motherly mindful mom to bring up your kids correctly.

CHAPTER THREE

AWARENESS OF YOUR THOUGHTS AND FEELINGS

To be mindful, you should be aware of your thoughts, which are an inner dialogue. Most people experience over seven thousand thoughts a day, with most of the thoughts repeating themselves. The ability to develop awareness of your thoughts puts you in a greater position to regulate, choose, or respond to events happening in your life. Your happiness depends on being fully aware of your inner dialogue as it directs your choices, which may either make you happy or otherwise. Additionally, your thoughts activate an emotion-driven process inside you. Your emotions or feelings are automatically triggered by you being aware of your thoughts and the fundamental beliefs driving them.

While your emotions may be triggered by your real-life experiences or the kids or family surrounding you. The feeling completely relies on your inner dialogue, which determines the type of emotion or feeling you finally experience. For instance, your child refused to do his homework, your thoughts will dictate if the action is pleasing or annoying, thereby determining your feeling of being sad, annoyed, puzzled, and so on.

Mindfulness requires you to be aware of your thoughts and feelings. When you are in control of your thoughts rather than your emotions, you will oversee your behaviors and thus be mindful. The first step to mindfulness is to transform your thoughts by developing self-awareness.

Emotional Awareness

Emotions or feelings are a system of complex molecules which command your body what to think, believe, and how to behave in certain situations. They act like "action signals" or "indicators" to guide you to your goal or vision. The success in overpowering life problems depends on your ability to experience your full package of emotions, enabling you to decide the most appropriate situation.

Pleasant emotions, such as happiness, confidence, and joy, tell you that you are achieving a certain goal in your motherhood life. However, they may be misleading at times as not all things that bring happiness may be good or healthy for your body, such as addictive foods, career choices, or substances. Therefore, you must be very careful about choosing the source of your happiness, and that of your kids.

It is absolutely normal to experience unpleasant emotions in our daily life as busy moms. Nevertheless, stress hormones are activated by unpleasant emotions such as shame, guilt, anger, hurt, and anxiety. Interestingly, unpleasant hormones enable us to understand a lot of information about our inner self through life experiences, which cannot be understood only through pleasant feelings. This is because when we are aware of our unpleasant feelings, we are in a good position to understand where we went wrong and what to correct to achieve success in our careers and the goals of our children.

Here are some of the techniques to be aware of our thoughts and feelings

1. Understand Situations which Trigger your Unpleasant Feelings

Select all the situations which trigger unpleasant feelings as a mom and note them in a notebook. It can be lateness at work or being abusive to your child. Start by working on the easily controlled triggers as you continue to handle the most challenging trigger. For instance, as a mother, you may start by working on an abusive kid and not allow your anger to overwhelm you. This requires patience and you have to practice patience to be successful. You may seek help from a professional counselor or a therapist to help you to overcome your emotional trigger.

2. Breathe deeply and slowly

On selecting the trigger that raises your emotions, reflect on it by taking 3 to 5 slow, deep breaths to help you to relax. Focus on your breathing while virtually scanning your entire body from head to toe, noticing and releasing any tension. Imagine yourself being in a safe place while reminding yourself of your emotions and thoughts. Observe your emotions while focusing on good emotions, and tell yourself that the emotions you may be experiencing are merely old pockets of energy and can change with time. This will enable you to be aware of your thoughts and feelings.

3. Try to Identify and Feel your Emotions

After breathing in and out deeply, you will feel relaxed and your selected trigger will be at the center of your mind. You should then pause and reflect on your feelings and sensations. Identify any feeling you may be experiencing as you are slowly taking deep breaths by asking yourself, "What am I feeling right now?". Write down the feelings and emotions on a piece of paper to identify your thoughts and feelings.

4. Accept your feelings and Emotions

You are the observer of your emotions. Emotions are energy, and what you are feeling are pockets of intensely charged energy, linked to past wounds. As the choice maker of your life, you may choose, if you wish, to breathe into any painful energy, notice it shift, move, and release. You can choose to affirm the power you have as a choice maker to accept your painful feelings, based on the circumstances of what you may be telling yourself. Calmly and confidently affirm, "I accept that I am feeling … at this moment."

Say this to yourself, silently or (when possible) aloud: "I can handle this emotion… I am strong and able to handle this wisely, easily, calmly."

A powerful way to get leverage on negative emotions is to remember a time when you experienced a similar emotion and successfully handled it. Since you handled it successfully in the past, you can handle it again in the present, and in the future, for that matter. Say to yourself, "I have done it in the past, I can now, and I can in the future." Repeat the affirmations as many times as necessary, to where you experience a shift in your emotional state and intensity. Allow yourself to take slow deep breaths throughout your body in between each repetition. Know that each time you handle the emotion, you add it to your repertoire of successes. This will grow and strengthen your confidence and future ability to handle, learn from, and turn fear-based emotions into assets.

5. Identify the cause of any emotions

Notice what you are thinking to yourself when you picture the triggering event, any toxic thinking patterns. Your thoughts automatically trigger emotions and physical sensations in your body. That's how the brain works.

Watch these thoughts from a safe distance, in which you are the objective observer, noticing yet not judging. Use the following visual. When a disturbing thought surfaces, imagine yourself on a luxurious speeding train, looking through the window, and observe any upsetting thoughts quickly zip by outside the window, while you sit comfortably in your seat in a safe place.

Record what you tell yourself in your self-talk in another column, next to the emotions and physical sensations you listed in steps 3 and 4 above.

6. Connect empathically to Understand and Validate your Experience

Remind yourself that, though other persons or situations may trigger painful feelings in you, they are never the cause. Your "self-talk" is the cause of all painful emotions you may feel, such as guilt or frustration, resentment or anger. What you tell yourself also causes the accompanying physical sensations in your body. This is good news. If how you "explain" your triggers to yourself (the specific situations or actions) is what causes upsetting emotions inside you, you can choose to change what you tell yourself. You can choose to think thoughts that calm and empower your confidence and ability to make informed choices.

Make a mental note that: this is really good news! It means you are the only person in charge of your emotional responses, thoughts, and actions. You can protect your happiness and peace of mind regardless of what situation you find yourself in. No one else can "make you" feel a certain way unless you allow it.

Understanding this creates statements that affirm and validate your experience, such as the following: "It makes sense that I feel overwhelmed because I'm telling myself, 'I'll never get this done… this is too much for me… I cannot handle it.'"

Thoughts trigger feelings, and feelings communicate vital information on how to best live your life to survive, and thrive. As you grow your awareness of what emotions and sensations you experience in response to certain thoughts, you will become more and more understanding of the strong connection between your words or thoughts (self-talk) and your emotions and physical sensations.

CHAPTER FOUR

MEDITATION

Meditation is a practice where an individual focuses their mind on a particular subject, or an activity to achieve a mentally and emotionally clear state. Meditation is a key component of mindfulness in your daily busy life as a mother. Mindfulness can be nurtured through the practice of mindful meditation, which enables us to be aware of the moment. Mindful meditation while sitting, enables us to become more present with ourselves, and in turn be more mindful.

Mindful meditation practice is simple and involves taking a good seat, paying attention to breathing, and letting your attention or concentration wander away by focusing on your mind. You can easily practice mindfulness by performing the following easy steps.

Sitting

You should find an open spot in your home away from too much clutter and too much noise. The room should be moderately lit with either natural light or electricity. You may choose to sit outside, just ensure there is no noise or any other distractions. Time yourself for about five to ten minutes for a start and extend steadily as you continue the process of meditation. Ultimately, you can meditate mindfully for about 45 minutes to an hour either early in the morning or late in the evening, depending on your schedule.

How to Sit?

There is a meditation posture that is perfect for mindful meditation as it allows you to focus your thoughts on your mind. The posture also stabilizes and relaxes your body, enabling you to easily meditate. You may also modify the posture if you have back injuries or other physical disabilities to match your condition. Here is the posture:

1. Sit on stable solid ground, whether a chair, a meditation cushion, or bench. The sit should not perch or hang backwards, to provide comfort.

2. Position your Legs. Position your legs comfortably by crossing them in front of you on a cushion on the floor. If you are on a sit, the bottom of your feet should touch the floor.

3. Straighten your upper body. Your upper body should be straight but not stiff. Your spine has a natural curvature, therefore, you shouldn't be straining to maintain an upward straight posture. Your head and shoulders should be naturally relaxed.

4. Position your arms parallel to your upper body. Let your left rest on top of your folded legs. Your upper arms should be at your sides and you should avoid straining any part of your body

5. Lower your chin and let your gaze fall gently downward. Lower your chin by facing downwards placing your eyelids a little bit lower, as you will close your eyes during meditation.

6. Maintain your Posture. Relax and bring your attention to your breathing or the sensations in your body.

7. Follow your Breath. Concentrate on your inhalation and exhalation by drawing your attention to the physical sensation of breathing. Follow the air moving through your nostrils to your chest and out through your mouth. Establish a point of concentration by counting the number of inhalations and exhalations. It is normal to occasionally lose your concentration, but you should slowly bring your concentration to the subject.

8. Pause your concentration before making any bodily adjustment. We sometimes have to make bodily adjustments, such as moving our bodies or

scratching an itch to attain comfort. When doing this, pause your concentration by shifting your mind from deep concentration to what you are experiencing in the moment.

9. Final Step. After completing the meditation process, gently lift your gaze and open your eyes if they were closed. Shift your mind to the present by noticing any sound in your surroundings.

Types of Mindful Meditation Techniques to Practice at Home

As we mentioned above, mindful meditation may help you steady your mind, enable you to be aware of your feelings and thoughts, and help you to manage stress that you may be facing in your daily life as a busy mom. Here are some mindful meditation techniques

1. Relaxed Breathing

You can use this type of meditation when you are feeling panicked, under pressure, or anxious, as it immediately relieves you of stress. Relaxed breathing is a simple exercise which activates the parasympathetic nervous system. Relaxed breathing lowers the heart rate and blood pressure instantaneously and quickly. When we inhale slowly and for a longer time, the body is signaled to relax, compared to when we exhale at a faster rate in a panic situation. When you are facing a difficult situation, just use relaxed breathing, as it tackles physical responses to acute stress, allowing us to be aware of our thoughts rather than reacting impulsively towards our kids when they are wrong.

Technique - Close your eyes and take a deep breath in for a count of four, and then exhale for a count of eight. As you inhale, visualize the movement of oxygen through your respiratory system. As you exhale, imagine any stress you've been holding float away. Repeat five times.

2. Mindful Breathing Meditation

Mindful breathing meditation takes seven minutes and can be performed daily to develop awareness of our thoughts and feelings, which are key to being mindful. In mindful breathing meditation, breath is employed as an object of meditation, enabling us to concentrate deeply on our thoughts and emotions. Mindful breathing strengthens our awareness of emotions and thoughts in our lives by forcing an inward awareness, enabling you to stay focused

Technique - Sit comfortably with a long, straight spine and find a slow, oceanic breath. Begin counting your inhales and exhales from one to ten (inhale one, exhale one; inhale two, exhale two; etc.). When you reach ten, start again but count back to one. Repeat this cycle five times. When you've completed five cycles of breath-counting, simply continue to breathe at this calm, steady pace for two-to-three minutes, visualizing the breath moving through the respiratory system and appreciating its physical relationship with the body.

3. Body Scan Meditation

This 5 minutes meditation can be used to build awareness of your body and discharge accumulated tensions after a long day of stressful work. A body scan meditation enables us to identify where our sad emotions and thoughts lie, thereby releasing them to relax and be mindful. Research has confirmed that regular body scan meditation develops mindfulness and significantly reduces the sleep conditions with the severity of stress and depression.

Technique - Sit or lie down in a comfortable position and take a few moments to find a calm, steady breath. Now, bring your awareness to sensations in the body, where you will spend several slow breaths on each focal point, beginning with the left toes and checking in with the left foot, left ankle, calf, knee, thigh, all the way through the left hip. When you notice an area of tension or discomfort, breathe into it, relaxing on the out-breath. Repeat through the right side. Follow with the pelvic region, abdomen and lower back, moving up through the torso and heart region. From there, follow and breathe through the sensations in the fingers, hands, wrists, up the arms, through the shoulders, neck, jaw, temples, ears, eyes, forehead, the crown of the head and skull.

CHAPTER FIVE
MINDFUL ACCEPTANCE

Acceptance of inner experience is an important component of mindfulness. It is the ability to accept negative emotions and thoughts without being over judgmental. Every day as moms, we undergo difficult life events from heavy tasks to caring for our kids leading to anxiety, stress, and depression. You may also experience secondary reactions which aggravate stressful feelings. When you are too judgmental of this stressful feeling, you automatically believe their negative predictions or views without questioning their accuracy, and you want to get rid of them as quick as possible. You will then see yourself as a weak character due to being too judgmental on your insecure thoughts and negative emotions. These secondary reactions worsen your emotional feeling and can only be resolved when you accept your inner emotions and thoughts. Mindful acceptance of your thoughts and feelings will make you view your current state as a temporary situation which gets better with time, and through it, you can avoid prolonging and exacerbating their impact on your life which may greatly limit your productivity.

Mindful acceptance can be conducted as an emotion efficacy therapy EET as a way of responding to emotional activation without judging, reacting or controlling the experience. Mindful acceptance is essential in our lives to enable us to tolerate negative distressing emotions, thereby reducing the stress we may be experiencing. Mindful acceptance can be learned through emotional awareness to clearly identify our emotions which we experience through sensations, feelings, thoughts, and urges. Mindful acceptance involves accepting situations, analyzing our thoughts, labeling our feelings, and noticing our urges.

How to Practice Mindful Acceptance

The first step in practicing mindful acceptance involves practicing in a non-activated state and steadily moving to an activated state involving your being aware of our emotions. Then for about ten minutes, practice nonjudgmental observation and acceptance of your current or previous emotional state. This will build your emotional efficacy muscle, making it easier for you to control your emotions when emotionally triggered by certain experiences in your life such as being angry at your kid.

Sit comfortably and close your eyes or focus on the spot in front of you. Spend a few minutes noticing sensations in your body. Scan your body to find sensation and just focus your attention on it. Try releasing your emotion by getting curious about it. Get curious about your emotion by noticing its shape and size and see whether it's moving or staying in the same place on your body. See if there's any temperature or tension in your feelings and ways in which you can soften it, or even lean into the sensation.

The next step is to identify the name of the feeling which goes with the sensation you are experiencing. Now spend a few minutes trying to notice your thoughts. You will be experiencing different types of thoughts; therefore, you should notice a thought which keeps flashing in your mind by simply saying, "There's a thought" or "Just thinking" and then choose the most appropriate thought. The key is just to notice your thought, but you should not get involved. Once you have identified a thought, you should let it go, return to the present moment, and wait for the next thought to arise. Keep on noticing and releasing your thoughts for about two minutes.

The final step entails seeing if there is an urge that goes with your sensations or thoughts. It could be an urge to do something, or not to do something. Notice what it's like not to act on the urge, but to just surf it.

Ways to Cultivate Mindful Acceptance

As we have stated above, mindful acceptance is the first step for any radical change involving your emotions and thoughts leading to mindfulness. If you do not acknowledge where you are and the current happenings, you can't move on appropriately from that point. Here are some of the ways to mindful acceptance.

Here are ways to cultivate acceptance

- If you are finding it difficult to accept an emotion or thought, gently state the label of the experience you aren't accepting. For example, if you're not accepting that you are angry, state in your mind to yourself, 'I'm feeling angry at the moment… I'm feeling angry.' In this way, you will be acknowledging your emotional state.

- Identify the part of your body which might be feeling tense and imagine your breath going into and out of the area of tightness. As you breathe in and out, console yourself by telling yourself, "'It's okay. It's already here…"

- Analyze how much you accept or acknowledge your current thoughts, feelings, and sensations on a scale of 1 to 10. Ask yourself what you need to do to increase your acceptance by 1, and then do it as best as you can.

- Develop curiosity about your experience. Consider: Where did this feeling come from? Where do I feel it? What's interesting about it? Your curiosity will lead to a little more acceptance.

Importance of Mindful Acceptance

Numerous studies have confirmed the importance of acceptance in being mindful. It is beneficial to accept your thoughts and feelings as they arise in response to stress. Most moms do not accept their feelings and thoughts and are always trying to judge or getting rid of them which further worsens the situation leading to stress or depression. Acceptance of inner experience is an aspect of mindfulness that can be learned by meditation and by consciously trying to be self-compassionate rather than being judged and self-critical. It may be impossible to prevent feelings and thoughts arising in everyday life, after all that's how we were all created, but if we can accept them and view them as just passing events, they will never hinder our happiness.

Furthermore, acceptance enables us to work through each unpleasant experience through an "allowing and letting" attitude when faced with a difficult situation. Interestingly, most moms know that it is important to be more caring, loving and accepting towards themselves and what they may be experiencing in terms of their thoughts or feelings. Most don't know how to practice mindful acceptance.

Being aware and accepting of every emotion or feeling which accompanies difficult situation you may be experiencing enables you to learn and relate differently to such experiences. With time, the practice of mindful acceptance will enable you to calmly handle unpleasant stressful experiences and avoid stress or, even worse, depression.

CHAPTER SIX

GRATITUDE AND JOY

Gratitude refers to a gracious acknowledgment of all that sustains us, a bow to our blessings, great and small, an appreciation of the moments of good fortune that sustain our lives every day. Gratitude is confidence in life. It is not sentimental, not jealous, nor judgmental. Gratitude does not envy or compare. It cares for every single life. As mothers, we have so much to be grateful for such as:

- Being home with our beautiful husband.

- Going for adventure on family-picnics, nature walks, and the zoo of course

- Watching our kids grow and start school

- Getting to know our wonderful neighbors and sharing our experiences.

- Developing our career and so much more

As our gratitude grows, it gives rise to joy. With joy, we experience the courage to rejoice in our own good fortune and in the good fortune of others. Joy flows naturally when our hearts are opened, and in it, we are not afraid of pleasure. It is not disloyal to the suffering of the world to honor the happiness we have been given.

Joy gladdens our heart just the same way gratitude does. We can be joyful for the people we love, for the moments of goodness, for sunlight and nature, and for the breath within our breast. As our joy grows, we soon discover happiness without cause.

Gratitude can be practiced by sitting quietly and at ease away. Allow your body to be relaxed and open as you breathe normally, maintaining a normal heartbeat. Then think of gratitude in your life. Think of how you have been able to care for your kids, family, and above all yourself to achieve a certain goal. You may practice gratitude by telling yourself words such as, "With gratitude, I have been blessed with kids" or "with gratitude, I have a beautiful family." And so on.

Continue to breathe gently while thinking of someone you care about, someone you easily rejoice for, it may be your kids and/or your husband. Picture them and feel the natural joy you have for their well-being, their success, and their happiness. With each breath, offer them your grateful, heartfelt wishes: You may wish them, "May you be happy". "May your joy increase" and much more.

Feel the sympathetic joy and caring in each phrase you are wishing happiness for the person in your mind. When you feel some degree of natural gratitude for the happiness of this loved one, extend this practice to another person you care about by reciting the same simple phrase to express your heart feelings and intentions.

Then gradually open the meditation to include neutral people, difficult people, and even enemies - until you extend sympathetic joy to all people in your life from your kids, husband, family to your workmates enabling you to be mindful in your busy life.

Cultivating Joy

Joy, which develops from gratitude as we have discussed above, is an important component of mindfulness practice. Joy enables us to be fully aware of our present life and also motivates us to embrace and overcome any suffering we may be experiencing. We can cultivate joy by using eight simple breaths, which you can employ when you are facing a stressful situation. In each breath, you will be saying a specific word to help you remember and focus your attention. Here are the eight breaths.

1. ***First Breath*** - *The first breath enables you to bring awareness to the sensation of your breathing. Pay close attention to the physical sensation of your breath as it moves in and out. Follow your in-breath and out-breath from the beginning to the end.*

2. ***Second Breath -*** *With the second breath, bring your attention to all the sensations in your entire body. Allow your awareness to completely fill your body and notice what you find. Some sensations will be pleasant, some unpleasant, and some neutral. See if you can allow yourself to feel these sensations without trying to change them at all. Pay special attention to any tension, heaviness, or agitation. The word for this breath is the body.*

3. ***Third Breath -*** *With the third breath, actively release all tension, heaviness, and agitation in your body. You can imagine that it is being washed out of you with your out breath. The word for this breath is release.*

4. ***Fourth Breath -*** *With the fourth breath, say to yourself, "May you have ease and lightness of body and mind." See if you can say this with your heart filled with love and generosity toward yourself. You are wishing yourself well and*

sending compassion to your body and mind. The word for this breath is love.

5. ***Fifth Breath** - With the fifth breath, notice if there are any cravings or aversions present in you. Is there any part of you that wants reality to be different than it is right now? Is there any way that you are not accepting or fighting against things-as-they-are? Just notice any cravings or aversions and let yourself feel them without trying to make them go away. They are not your enemy. They are a part of you that needs love and care. The word for this breath is cravings.*

6. ***Sixth Breath** - With the sixth breath, become aware that everything you need to be happy about is already present in this moment. All the conditions that are needed for peace, joy, and freedom are already here. In every moment of life, there are infinite reasons to suffer and infinite reasons to be happy. What matters is where we're putting our attention. Let's no longer ignore the*

positive conditions that are available at this moment. Problems do exist, but they are not all that exists. For this one breath, focus on everything in life that is good. We are no longer regretting the past or worrying about the future. We are here and present to the miracles of life. The word for this breath is letting go.

7. **Seventh Breath -** *With the seventh breath, become aware that you are alive. As you breathe, feel the energy of life moving through you. With this breath, we recognize the miracle of being alive. We become fully awake to the experience of being alive in the present moment, and we see what a precious thing this is. If you had just a few minutes to live, it would be so clear that 24 hours of life is incredibly precious. Let us not ignore this truth. The word for this breath is alive.*

8. **Eighth Breath -** *With the eighth breath, become aware of all the beauty within and around you. As soon as we let go of our desires and wake up to*

the present moment, we see that reality itself is indescribably beautiful. All our senses - sight, sound, smell, taste, touch, and mental perception - deliver this beauty to us like a precious gift. All we must do is enjoy. The word for this breath is beauty.

CHAPTER SEVEN

SUPPORTING OTHERS

Through mindfulness, you can support others as it makes you feel good about helping others. Empathy goes wrong when it leads to distress. Most people support others out of guilt, or the help might cause resentment, which makes us avoid helping people in the future. Sometimes, we might not be able to help people because absorbing the feelings of someone in trouble may lead us to turn away, more so if we can't handle such feelings or suffering. Nevertheless, compassion may enable us to try to assuage distress in others.

Research has shown that helping is most common among people who are able to maximize compassion while minimizing distress. Mindfulness making us in constant awareness of our thoughts, feelings, and surrounding leads to greater compassion, enabling us to support others more often. There are specific components of mindfulness, which determine our helping of certain behaviors. These are the present-focused attention and non-judgmental acceptance to predicting our helping behavior.

While helping others, we are likely to experience emotions such as joy, elation, and compassion, making us feel better about helping others and could lead others to engage in more supportive behavior. It is important to note that mindful sharing starts with you as a mom and, therefore, you should have a strong personal mindfulness practice. You, therefore, need to continue developing your mindfulness with intensive routine practice such as meditation, breath, gratitude, and joy as discussed in the previous topics.

We can only share mindfulness with our kids, families or those surrounding us through incorporating mindfulness in our daily busy lives, and not through doing it from ideas or concepts we have read in a book such as this one. You must practice every idea.

Self-care through mindfulness is also critical in helping others. It may be difficult to master the art of self-care which spans across domains of mental, spiritual and emotional care. Self-care involves various techniques or routines and may vary from people to people. For instance, for you to care for your physical body, you may exercise regularly by taking regular nature walks with your husband or your dog or you may visit the gym quite often. To nurture your emotional life, you may spend time with your kids or family, read a novel or watch a movie that stimulates your positive emotion. To nurture your mental care, you may explore interests beyond those related to your career by learning something new every day. Spiritual life can be developed by engaging in prayers, reading or watching inspirational stories and mindfulness practices daily.

It is important for you as a mom to cultivate your well-being as it is beneficial for your children. Without self-care, our well-being will be in question and we will be depleted of energy and we may not be fully available to provide our kids the much-needed parental care or even support them. With an increasing social change, coupled with a stressful life, we are increasingly being socially disconnected from our children which is dangerous for their development and well-being. As mothers, we are responsible for our children and the importance of nurturing them until their future as adults. When we are mindful and care for ourselves, we act as good examples to our children, who will also learn to be mindful, calm, peaceful, open-hearted and thoughtful through us.

CHAPTER EIGHT

PRACTICING COMPASSION

Mindfulness and compassion can help us cultivate and maintain emotional supportiveness of our kids and those surrounding us. Mindfulness involves cultivating a state of present-centered awareness with an attitude of openness and curiosity coupled with being less judgmental. Compassion refers to a motivational understanding which recognizes our common human suffering, enabling us to open-heartedly care for others. By cultivating compassion, we are able to recognize the behaviors of our kids or those within our circle. Research shows that cultivating empathy through compassion meditation affects brain regions, which make you more sympathetic to other peoples' mental states.

Mindfulness is not just about paying attention, but also how to pay attention and be compassionate. A kind attentive person is not frustrated when their mind wanders away, instead they become curious about what their mind meanders about, holding this experience in compassionate awareness. Therefore, instead of being angry at your mind, or impatient with yourself, you could inquire gently and benevolently into what it felt like to be frustrated or impatient. Through this, you grow kindness towards yourself coupled with a sense of interest and curiosity in your life experiences. As a mother, you should infuse your compassion in your young child saying, "I care about you".

The connection between Mindfulness and Compassion

Understanding the connection between mindfulness and compassion is important as it will enable you to embrace your kids, family, and yourself with greater kindness and care. Instead of trying to control or judge our experience, we should take an interest in it with the attitude of how we pay attention.

Research has shown that mindfulness increases empathy and compassion for others and for oneself and that such attitudes are good for your well-being. When we practice mindfulness, we are simultaneously strengthening our compassion skills, since mindfulness is not about sharpening attention.

However, it is important to note that self-compassion does not always mean that we should be filled with happiness and loving kindness. It simply means that our awareness of what's happening should always be kind and compassionate, such that even when you feel angry or frustrated, you should embrace your situation with compassionate awareness. When we handle our stressful situation in this way, we are better able to be with it, see it clearly and respond appropriately to it, as we will be strengthening the skills that help us extend compassion towards others.

The other way mindfulness cultivates compassion is through interconnectedness. Mindfulness cultivates interconnectedness and clear seeing, leading to greater compassion and understanding of the mysterious web in which we are all woven.

Mindfulness cultivates empathy and compassion by guarding against the feelings of stress and busyness, which makes us focus more on ourselves and lessen the needs of other people. The Good Samaritan experiments conducted in the 1970s suggested that people are not inherently morally insensitive. However, when we are stressed or depressed we tend to lose our deepest values. Mindfulness enables us to stay connected with our current situation in the present moment, regardless of the time, increasing our empathy and compassion.

How to Practice Compassion as a Mother

Research has shown that practicing compassion for others also benefits you. As a mother trying to balance a career and family may be challenging and you may end up feeling guilty, overwhelmed, and inadequate while striving to be "perfect" and successful in your chosen career. Our culture today creates an illusion of always being perfect in people's minds. However, the truth is that imperfection is an essential human trait and every mother undergoes the same feeling as you.

To practice self-compassion, you first need to become observant of people's lives, which may be fulfilling, tedious, joyful and frustrating. It is important to note that not everyone is perfect, nor do they have a perfect life. When you start letting go of the need to try to be the "perfect" mom, you liberate yourself from this illusion, which is the first step to practicing self-compassion.

A common thought I am sure you can all relate to is, "I'm a bad mother." It is this kind of judgmental thought which leads you to start comparing yourself to other moms. If you bring a sense of acceptance and mindful awareness to thoughts such as this, you can choose to respond with compassion by saying something like, "I hear you, you feel pretty bad right now and it's ok to feel this way", or something like, "You're managing a huge task here, juggling so many balls, occasionally you're going to drop one and that's ok".

By responding this way, you're not only practicing kindness and forgiveness, you're giving yourself permission to be accepting of your situation and perceived failures and acceptance is key to your happiness. It is through this acceptance the weight of judgment is lifted and the vicious cycle of feeling inadequate and overwhelmed is broken.

Unfortunately, there are misunderstandings surrounding the practice of self-compassion which prevents people from trying it out for themselves. Some of these misunderstandings suggest self-compassion is a form of weakness, self-pitying, or an attitude which is indulgent. In truth self-compassion isn't any of these things. To practice self-compassion requires courage and great inner strength.

Try the following exercise to have a taste of what it is like to practice self-compassion.

Mindfulness for Busy Moms

- Take five minutes for the exercise and observe how quickly you can feel a shift in your mindset from feelings of inadequacy, guilt or to be overwhelmed, to feelings of balance and calm.

- Begin to reflect on a situation which is currently, or has recently, caused you upset.

- A situation perhaps where you dropped one of those many balls you've been juggling...

- Close your eyes and start to pay attention to all the whirling thoughts attached to that situation.

- Try not to control the thoughts or push them away. Simply allow yourself to hear and experience them fully in this present moment.

- While doing this if it's comfortable to do so, place your hand on your heart or on your shoulder, the way you would if you were comforting a friend.

- Think about things you would say to a friend to offer them words of comfort, then repeat these things to yourself.

- Observe how cruel your own thoughts can be, and then notice how differently you would speak to your friend. You wouldn't dream of repeating some of the things you often say to yourself!

Also, pay close attention here to how it feels when you offer yourself compassion. People can occasionally feel awkward or uncomfortable initially because it's a way of behaving towards yourself that you're not used to, but just try to go with that feeling and don't forget to give yourself compassion for that too.

CHAPTER NINE

DEALING WITH STRESS

Stress is a harmful response to a collection of physiological changes which occur when you face a perceived threat or in situations which demand to outweigh your resources for you to significantly cope with the situation. Stress triggers our fight-or-flight response, shutting down the executive function in our brain and filling us with adrenaline and cortisol. In our daily lives as mothers, we experience stress from different situations such as juggling work and taking care of our children.

It is normal to experience stress and may sometime be good for you since some form of pressure develops and prepares to meet certain challenges in our lives. Stress should not be a cost of success such that you must undergo stress to achieve your goals. Research published in the Popular Science magazine revealed that chronic stress could be dangerous for our health. Chronic stress affects various parts of our bodies from the health of our nervous, cardiovascular, and digestive systems to our cells, immunity and general body metabolism. People react differently to stress. Most people have their own tested techniques for managing stress such as a good sleep, going to the gym or going to a pub, which is not advisable.

One way to deal with stress is through mindfulness and meditation. Mindfulness has been proven to not only reduce stress, but also to gently build an inner strength so that future stress conditions or stressors does not affect our happiness and physical well-being. If we handle stress more mindfully, we tend to be less reactive and focus on the solution to the stressor rather being more judgmental on the small details causing the stress. When we lack mindfulness in dealing stress, we will tend to be more reactive and the stress we may be facing will develop into depression, which is far worse.

One of the key practices in dealing with stress is to develop a strong mind strength through mindful meditation involving deep awareness of our thoughts, feelings, and what is happening around us. Mind strength is the ability to very quickly and easily shift out of a reactive mode and become fully present at the moment, experiencing the full force of your emotions even as you recognize that they are temporary and will soon fade out.

Mindful meditation practice can affect the amount of activity in the brain i.e. the amygdala which is responsible for regulating emotions. When the amygdala is relaxed, the parasympathetic nervous system engages to counteract anxiety response. The heart then lowers the heartbeat rate as breathing deepens and its rate slows, and the body is initiated to stop releasing the stress hormone, cortisol, and adrenaline into the bloodstream. With time, mindful meditation thickens the bilateral, prefrontal right-insular region of the brain which is responsible for optimism and a sense of well-being, making it as spacious as possible. This part of the brain is also responsible for creativity and curiosity coupled with the ability to be reflective. With an increased brain space, you are ready to control your thoughts and emotions, thus being able to deal with stress effectively.

As a mother, mindful meditation is also important for your kids to deal with stress effectively. Kids face a wide range of stressors ranging from stressful academics to social situations and interestingly, they may not be able to tell or know if they are stressed. Therefore, it is important for moms to monitor their behaviors and tell if they are facing stress. You should help your children learn mindful meditation and thereby reduce stress by recognizing their stressors and refocusing their attention on what is actually upcoming rather than the past. Kids, when faced with stress, should meditate for about five minutes daily as it retains their mind from overthinking, making it easier for them to refocus their attention to other issues thus limiting the stress they may be experiencing. Additionally, mindfulness helps create a compassionate attitude towards themselves and others. Dealing with stress in kids is important to protect them from developing mental illness and further helps their social functioning.

Here are some examples we experience in our daily lives and how to manage them through meditation and mindfulness.

1. Burnout

Burnout arises from working for long hours without a rest or without replenishing your energy. Burnout is a killer common in big-minded people who have big plans, big visions or big goals. One of the best ways to prevent burnout is through meditation. When you meditate, you trigger the relaxation response, which is a physical state of deep rest that changes the physical and emotional responses to stress to the opposite of the fight or flight response.

Mindfulness also gives you access to a deeper level of your own awareness, thereby enabling you to handle stressful situations more easily. Mindful meditation rejuvenates your energy and reserves and creates space for fresh thinking and perspective. Burnout may be very rare at home and usually occurs at workplaces. At work, while experiencing burnout, meditation is one the best preemptive action. Learning to deal with stress through mindfulness meditation will restore your energy and help you to focus on your work while centering your mind and expanding your awareness beyond the stressful situation.

2. Stress Addiction

Stress addiction is a condition where an individual is so used to pressure that they are unable to work without any stressful condition as an initiator. Stress can be beneficial as it propels us to work or perform a certain task to avoid that stressful condition. For instance, you may be forced to work not out of good will or passion but, to cater to the needs of your kids or family. Stress then develops and becomes chronic stress if we are unable to cater to the needs of our kids or manage the task assigned to us. Although stress can be beneficial, most often it is acute or chronic and many of us struggle to deal or manage it, leading to a great negative impact in our lives, such as depression.

We can deal with stress addiction effectively through meditation. Meditation and stress are opposite, therefore regular mindful meditation helps you to cultivate access to the dimension of yourself that is free from anxiety, worry, and the pressure of deadlines. As you practice meditation and access your inner thoughts and feelings, you will let go of any stressors and develop a preference for calm and centered composure over stress. Therefore, through mindful meditation, you will avoid stress addiction as you will be propelled to work through an inner drive rather than meditation.

3. Focus your Mind

Mindful meditation enables you to center your mind. Chronic stress disrupts your focus by dividing your mind. Your mind needs to be steady to care for your children, and at the same time advance your career. A contrary belief of focusing your mind is to stop your thoughts from racing in your mind. Instead, mindful meditation teaches us to be the case with the unpredictable turbulence of your mind. Through mindful meditation, you cannot lose focus and continuous practice will build a sense of positivity and confidence in you, therefore, you will easily overcome a stressful situation and focus on the present.

4. Rediscovering Yourself

Mindful meditation enables you to rediscover yourself when faced with stress. Most people, when faced with stress, lose themselves by spreading themselves too thin, limiting their space to solve their issues. With meditation, you are returned to the center of your mind where you will be able to gain the confidence and conviction to maneuver a stressful experience. Meditation slows down your thinking and provides enough calm space to come which works in solving the stress and returning you to your normal life. For instance, when you are faced with a stressful condition from work or stress from kids, you might not be able to solve the problem causing the stress by approaching different people to help solve your personal problems. You will just generate more stress, resentment, and other strong emotional responses, which may lead to depression. Always employ mindful meditation to rediscover yourself, stay centered, and come up with the most appropriate action to solve the problem causing stress.

How to Mindfully Meditate to Solve your Stress

1. First, think of a current challenge you may be facing in your life that causes you stress. Don't think of your biggest problem but just a small situation, which you will be able to solve at the moment.

2. Vividly bring the situation to your mind. Imagine being in the stressful situation and all the difficulties associated with it causing stress.

3. Try to feel the stress in your body. Look out for stress signals which include physical tension, faster heart rate, butterflies in your stomach, sweating usually in the hands and so on. They vary widely in individuals.

4. Convert the stress signal you have identified into emotions. Notice where the emotion might be coming from in your body and label the emotion if you can. Try as much as you can to locate emotion coupled with the sensation.

5. Next, bring your mindful attitudes to the emotion, which include friendliness, curiosity, and acceptance.

6. Try to gently place your hand on the location of the sensation to represent kindness.

7. While breathing, feel the sensation by promoting present-moment awareness and mindful attitudes with your experience.

8. Meditate for about five minutes and bring it to a close upon finishing.

Tips to Help Remain Calm when Dealing with Your Difficult Child

It is certain that you may experience constant fights with

your child, but how do you stay calm? It is important to stay calm when your child is anxious, upset, or angry since your calm is worth half the battle and your children develop their personalities from your behavior. It is important to note that all emotions are acceptable, but all behaviors are not. As mothers, we should accept our emotions to avoid passing them out to our kids or family in an abusive manner.

It may be challenging to stay calm with the kids and sometimes our emotions may get out of hand no matter how we try to control it. This is because, amid anger, our brain becomes overloaded with emotions, which initiates reactivity in the form of yelling, screaming and shutting down, making you unable to deal with your kids.

Parenting is an emotional experience contributed to by interaction with our kids, triggering a variety of our own feelings such as frustration, happiness, helplessness, disappointment, confusion, and rage, just to name a few. The feelings can quickly escalate, leaving triggering an appropriate action based on the situation. In most cases, these actions emotionally hurt our children, therefore we should try to control our feelings rather than the feeling being in control of us by acting calmly. Here are some ways to maintain your cool while dealing with your kid.

1. Think Differently

If you can think differently about your children and understand that they are just acting their age, you will be less angry at them. You should practice tolerance, patience, attitude, and outlook when dealing with your difficult child. For instance, if your child swears at you, it is almost certain that you will feel angry, but you should remember that they are kids before taking any appropriate action. This should not be confused with allowing bad behavior but to find a way to correct them without being angry at them. Every mother should find a way of correcting their child gently and calmly without being over-reactive or angry. If we are used to blaming our kids for our feelings and reactions, they will grow up learning to blame others for their actions and will not learn to take responsibility for their actions.

2. Change your Perspective

If you can change your perspective of your children, you will be less angry at them. No matter how our kids make us annoyed, mad or frustrated, we should always remember that they are acting their age. Our annoyance can be controlled through patience, tolerance and a positive attitude. Kids will always test limits by breaking rules as this is part of their developmental stage, which can be annoying and frustrating for us, but it is important to maintain our cool by understanding them. Our job as mothers is, therefore, to guide our kids to better behavior by offering them natural consequences, not to blame them for behavior.

It is important to find ways to be less angry at our kids. If we are responsible for our feelings and actions, they will be more likely to be able to do the same.

3. Establish your Feelings

It is important to identify your feelings whether it is frustration, irritation or hurt. Identify each feeling as your own by saying to yourself, "When I see my kid doing X,

Y or Z, I feel — because I —". For instance, "When I see my kid not helping around the house, I feel furious because I feel ineffective as a parent. I'm scared he will never be responsible and guilty that I have not done my job"

When we identify our feelings, we acknowledge and accept our own feelings, we can then start doing the work of soothing them, understanding them, changing them, processing them and releasing them. We will then be able to control our feelings more effectively making them not spill into others. It is the responsibility of us as mothers to identify our underlying feelings of fear, inadequacy or shame which are easily triggered by our kids. It is tempting to blame our kids for triggering our feelings rather than striving to control our emotions. Always remember that our kids only trigger the feeling within us, but they do not cause the feeling. Therefore, it is wrong to blame our kids for the feelings within us as it's our responsibility to work with our own feelings.

4. Control your Breath and Think

A deep controlled breath can calm you down once you are red-hot inside. Always talk to your child once you are frustrated as they will know how to deal with the difficult feeling. For instance, you may say to them, "I'm frustrated right now, so I'm going to take a few deep breaths, calm myself down and figure out how to best deal with this situation" or "we can talk later because I am frustrated right now". Not only does this enable you to control your emotions but also teaches your kids to calm down when they are angry at you for certain reasons.

When you pause and take a deep breath, you bring down the levels of adrenaline in the body. When your child swears to you, your body feels emotionally threatened, thus sending a "fight" or "flight" response to the brain, which in turn empowers your muscles with energy. This sequentially leads us to perform actions such as whipping or throwing words at our kids which we later regret. By pausing and breathing deeply, we alleviate the "fight" and "flight" response, enabling us to solve the problem effectively and calmly.

Keeping calm when you are angry is an essential skill for any mother who cares for her child. Nevertheless, calmness is contagious, and if you learn to be calm, you will definitely create a calm family.

CHAPTER TEN

MANAGING ANGER

As mothers, how often do we come home tired from work in a happy mood and suddenly change our peaceful mood into anger! We start shouting and getting angry at our kids for various reasons. Maybe they have broken something. They may not have done their homework, or you may arrive home late, and your partner hasn't cooked any food, and your anger might rise up. Anger is not necessarily a bad emotion. It's a normal emotion which enables us to rectify an issue we may be experiencing. Nevertheless, we should not get used to blowing up regularly as it could negatively affect the development of your kids. It is also quite embarrassing to show that we are unable to hold our temper and can be both hurtful to both your children and you. Anger is an inner alarming system which tells us that something is wrong, or off balance, when an event has not matched with our expectations, beliefs or our spirit. Anger has several drawbacks. First, it destroys your inner peace and distorts your view on reality. Your anger triggers include situations that you feel are unfair or unjust, actions that cause you to feel disrespected, hurt, frustrated, or disappointed, or things you simply don't like, such as irritations and annoyances from your children.

Using Mindfulness to Control Your Anger

One way in which we can manage our anger is through mindfulness. If we could stop for a moment to fully feel the emotion when we first notice our anger, we could be able to control our anger. When you are angry, try to notice how your body feels. Maybe you feel some sort of tightness in your chest, your body tenses and heats up followed with the shallowing of your breath. When you practice mindfulness, you will stop to notice these sensations in your body. Common anger sensations or impulses include:

- Feeling threatened
- Feeling irritable
- Ruminating on the anger trigger
- Raising your voice
- Feeling fear or jealousy
- Fantasizing about revenge or aggression
- Feeling unsafe
- And much more

After identifying these sensations through mindfulness, it is eminent that you will accept and acknowledge these and later let them go, preventing anger from engulfing your mind. When we recognize and accept our feelings and simply observe our thoughts, we are in a much better position to make a conscious choice about how best to respond to all the daily annoyances we encounter. Anger is an emotional energy which needs to be processed for our emotional health, otherwise it will continue to recycle itself, always resurfacing. With mindfulness, we can easily recognize the internal signals or clues that anger is rising within us and we can easily switch to a mindset of curiosity and self-investigation about what our anger is directing us to do and then hopefully be able to control our anger before directing us to act appropriately. There are two main techniques to control sensations or impulses leading to anger. They are anger dumpers and anger withholders.

Anger Dumpers - *They are essential to keep us calm by preventing our bodies from acting due to the anger feeling. It involves closing the eyes and taking slow, deep breaths for about five minutes. We then convince ourselves not to react but rather to relax with the feeling within us. Being alone can be important while using this technique.*

Anger withholders - *This technique enables us to be aware of our feelings and thoughts as they are essential in avoiding anger. Always remember that thoughts come before feelings, therefore, being aware of our thoughts can help prevent the anger feeling. This technique involves various exercises such as gripping your opposite forearm in each hand and hugging yourself tight while keeping your eyes open and focusing in staying in our body. Here are some of the ways you can employ mindfulness to control your anger.*

1. Being aware of the Physical Sensation of Anger in your Body

Try to identify the sensations in your stomach, face, and chest as we mentioned above. Notice the rate of your heartbeat and breathing. Observe if your fists or jaw are clenched.

2. Breathe Deeply

Breathe deeply into the physical sensation of your body. You may close your eyes and count up to ten breaths.

Imagine your breath entering through your nostrils into your chest and out through your mouth.

3. Sensational Awareness.

As you continue to breathe, try as much as possible to be aware of your senses. Bring a sense of gentleness and kindness to your feelings of anger. Try to view anger as an opportunity to comprehend your feelings and how breath may have a cooling effect on the burning inside you.

4. Identify your Thoughts

You should then notice or identify your thoughts through deep meditation. Then you should let go of the thoughts such as, "It's not fair" or "I'm not having this". Your thoughts and feelings are co-relative and by letting go of these thoughts, your feeling of anger also fade away.

5. Communicate

Communication is key to coping with anger. When you communicate your feelings to your kids or the other person by beginning with, "I" rather than "you", you will rediscover yourself and stay aware of your own feelings. You will then let go of any aggression which greatly contributes to anger, enabling you to converse harmoniously.

CHAPTER ELEVEN

MEANING AND PURPOSE OF LIFE

Mindfulness can enable us to rediscover the meaning and purpose of life. As busy moms, we are stuck in one routine, which might make our lives lose meaning and purpose. While working for about ten hours per day, it is inevitable that there will be a time where you will lose the meaning of life by asking yourself, "What is the meaning of all this?" You can experience the feeling of being alive again through mindfulness. While practicing mindfulness, we can find the meaning of our lives by slowing down to notice our thoughts, choices, and actions for what we have done in a day. For example, you may notice the example you are setting to your kids through your actions. It is important to understand that the meaning of life differs from one person to another and from day to day, therefore what really matters in your life is not the meaning but the purpose of your life at a given moment. While it may be difficult to define the purpose of life, most psychologists believe that life has four purposes, namely:

- Learning life's lessons

- Finding your career and calling

- Discovering your life path

- Life continuity

Many people believe that the purpose of life arises from special gifts or talents which set you aside from all other people. Purpose also grows from the connection with other people from whom we may relate. While purpose may vary largely according to a person, it is adaptive and evolves and helps human beings survive today.

Using Mindfulness to Discover the Purpose of your Life

Mindfulness dictates that we should forgive those who we have wronged by letting go negative thoughts about them. To find our life purpose, we need something to feel rather than just an intellectual pursuit. Research shows that certain emotions such as awe, gratitude, and altruism, not only promote our well-being, but also foster a sense of purpose. Awe makes us connected with something we think is larger than us, probably your creator. This connection provides a sense of emotional foundation which cultivates purpose. Awe by itself does not give your life a purpose, as you will need a sense of drive to identify your life purpose. Generosity and gratitude give your life a sense of drive which is equivalent to purpose. People who express gratitude for the blessings they have in their lives are more likely to have found life purpose. Altruistic behaviors such as volunteering or donating money have been established to have a greater sense of purpose in life.

Mindful meditation can help us to discover life's purpose. Meditation allows us to connect with our inner voice and find out the destiny of our life. Our thoughts are able to settle much more easily through meditation, which is just the beginning to discovering life's purpose. A virtual body scan through meditation makes you discover whether or not your life has a purpose. Reflective meditation allows you to find life's purpose by sinking into deeper consciousness and lets your inner voice identify your purpose. We identify our purpose in life by looking inward to connect with what fulfills us and feels right.

As a mom, it is important to identify the purpose of your life as it fosters the relationship between you and your kids. When you lack purpose in life, your relationship is hugely impacted as you are absent in the relationship with your kids or husband. Purpose also unlocks your true potential as you will be able to realize your natural talents. The passion for life or zeal is only realized through identifying your life purpose, thereby making a real contribution to the lives of your kids.

CONCLUSION

How to Start Being Mindful Today

As discussed in the previous chapter, being mindful takes time and it's not an overnight process. Mindful living does not just entail mindful breathing or meditation. It involves several other routines, such as being mindful of the body's physical sensations along with being aware of our thoughts, feelings or emotions always. Additionally, mindfulness should be incorporated into common daily activities such as walking, driving, cleaning and many more. However, starting to live a mindful life can be easy and all it takes is to carry out mindful activities more often. At first, mindful practices may be hectic, but with time, they become part of your life. Here are some ways to start living a mindful life today

- Pause and notice your breathing. Imagine the flow of breath from your nostrils to your chest into your belly and out through your toes.

- Always be aware, both mentally and physically, of the activities you are undertaking at a certain moment by tuning your senses. For instance, if you are bathing your kid, notice the feeling of his skin or the texture of his hair.

- Be aware of your thoughts and feelings but you should not be judging them, only notice.

- Identify the activities in which your mind tends to wander away (zone out) e.g. when driving, washing dishes, texting and many more. Then, train your mind to be more aware during these activities.

- Practice random mindful check-ins, which involve meditating upon your physical body for quite some time randomly.

- Practice listening mindfully to anybody speaking. Mindful communication involves being fully present when the other person is talking through being aware of your thoughts, emotions or bodily sensations.

How to Create Habits of Mindfulness and Meditation and Stick to Them

It is important that you come up with meditation habits as they are essential to living mindfully. Mindfulness is a practice which will later develop into a habit, and in turn, you will live a mindful life. Here are some ideas for creating habits of mindfulness and meditation.

1. Develop a Consistent Meditation Schedule

A meditation schedule is very effective in creating mindfulness habits as they train your body to become adjusted to meditation at specific times. If you don't have a meditation schedule, you will keep procrastinating, coming up with excuses, thereby you may end up creating a bad habit. A suggestion is to meditate once a day in the morning after waking up before starting your day.

2. Identify a Specific Meditation Spot

At your house, identify a perfect spot for meditation away from distractions such as noise or excessive light. A meditation spot contributes to making meditation a daily habit as it's the perfect place to find peace and silence each day. After establishing a perfect meditation spot, place a meditation pillow and remove distractors such as computer or sound system and anything obstructing you from sitting

3. Always start you Meditation with a Breath

You should always start your meditation with a simple deep breath. Breathing calms your mind, bringing your thoughts and feelings to your present state, essential for building the foundation of your meditation practice. Breath is also super easy, and a meditation beginner can easily and quickly invoke meditation.

4. Combine Mindfulness in your Daily Activities

When you practice mindfulness in your daily life, you can easily form a daily habit of meditation compared to just focusing on meditation. The more you are exposed to something, the more easily you form a habit. Therefore, you should practice mindfulness more often as it will further support the habit of meditation

Mindful Things to do Everyday

These are activities which we undertake daily, incorporating mindfulness in them. Such activities are discussed below.

Cleaning

Cleaning involves repetitive action and can be the perfect activity to incorporate mindfulness. When you apply mindfulness principles in cleaning and organizing your home, you will not only end up getting a cleaner house, but you will also learn to find meaning in mundane chores and ordinary moments. Cleaning also offers you an opportunity to practice mindfulness. Whether it is wiping the windows, washing the dishes, mopping the floor or wiping countertops, you will be able to invoke a greater peace, coupled with the satisfaction characteristic of mindfulness.

Walking

Mindful walking involves short walks each day, such as walking from your car to work or home, or walking to the store and many more. Mindful walking complements meditation and requires you to be consciously aware and moving in the environment rather than sitting down, meditating with eyes closed. Mindful walking has been proven to strengthen your concentration, making you more aware of your feelings and thoughts, allowing you to be present in the moment.

Driving

If you commute to work daily, driving can be a great opportunity to practice mindfulness. It is obvious that while driving, you cannot close your eyes nor focus on your breath. Mindful driving can be used as meditation in several ways, such as noticing your attitude. For instance, when someone immediately pulls in front of you or practicing being more aware of other traffic surrounding you, practicing controlling your anger, practicing a fuller mindfulness of your body by stopping at every stop light and much more. If you take public transport instead, you can practice mindfulness by wishing those around you well, expressing kind loving towards them.

Showering

A daily shower is a perfect opportunity to practice mindfulness. While alone and hot water running over you, you can observe a habitual pattern of thinking by sinking into deep meditation. Feel the water hitting your body and notice the thoughts running through your mind. Showering also offers us an opportunity to come to our senses by perhaps feeling the scent of the soap on our skin or the water against our skin. When we come to our senses, we are then aware of our thoughts and feelings.

Cooking

Mindful cooking is a great way to practice mindfulness. It is a very satisfying experience to prepare meals with awareness, and you will end up cooking very delicious meals. Mindful cooking begins right at the meal planning stage. Ensure that you are aware of what you are going to eat on that day. As you choose the meal you will prepare that day, shop for the ingredients and hit your kitchen, with each step in the recipe being an opportunity to practice mindfulness.

Mindfulness has changed the lives of millions of people around the world. Lives have been able to find meaning and purpose again through an awareness of their thoughts and feelings. As a mother, it is important to practice mindfulness, as it enables you to raise your children correctly amongst the other benefits we have discussed in this book. We hope this book has been instrumental, enabling you to comprehend all about mindfulness, and that it will mark the next phase of your life in beginning to live a mindful life.

BONUS

Free e-book

Now you know the power of mindfulness and meditation. But it doesn't change the fact you are still busy and have no time for yourself. I want to help you, so I created an e-book about staying organized. It will help you declutter your house and manage your time more effectively. I'm giving it to you completely for FREE. It's a gift. All you have to do is type the link below into your browser.

https://bit.ly/2sCe4El

Made in the USA
Columbia, SC
11 November 2018